SUZUKI

SUZUKI

Geoff Aspel

Arco Publishing, Inc. *New York*

Published by Arco Publishing, Inc.
215 Park Avenue South, New York, NY 10003

© Geoff Aspel 1984

Library of Congress Catalog Card Number: 83-73616
ISBN 0-668-06164-2 Hardcover Edition
ISBN 0-668-06171-5 Paper Edition

Printed in Italy

Contents

Beautiful girls and beautiful bikes – the two seem to go together perfectly. This is the mighty GSX road burner.

1 History to 1977

The giant Suzuki motor-cycle factory, now one of the largest in the world, started over sixty years ago in Japan making spinning looms. Now, with a large share of the motor-cycle market, they have branched out again into cars, vans, trucks, outboard motors and many other types of manufacturing.

It is, however, for motor cycles that Suzuki is best known, and their appearance in the two-wheel market started in June 1952, with an odd little machine, called the 'Power Free'. Only a few months before the 36cc single two-stroke went on sale did the company actually make its first tests – an indication of the speed at which Suzuki were to develop in the years to come.

Only nine months later, Suzuki launched yet another machine onto the market – the 'Diamond Free'. This was a simple, easy to maintain engine which was mounted onto the front wheel of a bicycle. Suzuki employees who had been trained to make looms, now found themselves making motor-cycle parts, some by hand.

By May 1954, Suzuki had made their first 'proper' motorcycle, the 'Colleda co'. The company thought that as the Diamond Free was now selling close to 5000 units per month, they were now ready to move on to greater, and more powerful things.

The Colleda co was a 90cc four-stroke, single-cylinder lightweight and was an immediate success. It won an important national Japanese race in its first year of production, ensuring its future.

By June of 1954, the company decided that it should change its name from Suzuki Jidosha Kogyo (meaning Suzuki Automotive Industries), to Suzuki Motor Co. Ltd, the name it uses to this day.

March 1955 saw the introduction of the company's largest machine. Called the Colleda cox, it was a 125cc four-stroke, single-cylinder bike with more modern styling. Also launched at the same time, was a redesigned version of the now popular two-stroke Colleda, called the Colleda st. This had better and more sophisticated suspension and lighting, and sold in huge numbers. To meet the demands of the market, it was now bored out from 90 to 125cc.

The foresight of Suzuki's engineers was made clear when the last models of the Colleda, made in May 1959, were fitted with electric starters, leaving their European competitors dumbfounded.

Early in 1956, Suzuki technicians were spending more and more time developing a completely new competition machine. Based on the hugely successful Colleda, it was to become known as the TT, and was the forerunner of the Grand Prix machines which were later to dominate racing. A high-performance machine for its time, it could touch over 80mph and was considered very advanced with its indicators, and built-in, four-speed gearbox. It was capable of out-performing machines with far more powerful engines, despite producing only 18bhp from its 250cc, twin-cylinder, two-stroke engine.

By 1958, Suzuki Motor Co. Ltd had 50, 125 and 250cc machines in its range, and in May, it launched the 'Suzumoped SM', using the well-established Mini Free power plant mounted in a spine-type frame.

In October of that year, Suzuki were to introduce their corporate 'S' logo which was to be used on all their machines and is still used by the motor-cycle division to this very day.

June 1960 was a milestone for Suzuki. It was then that they took their factory-prepared 125cc Colleda racers to the Isle of Man to compete in the lightweight TT. Although they did not win at their first attempt, they managed a respectable fifteenth, sixteenth and eighteenth places, and British and European spectators were very impressed with these strange-looking and strange-sounding Japanese machines. Suzuki, like the other Japanese manufacturers, were anxious to show the buying public that their machines were fast and yet reliable.

At the beginning of the next decade, Suzuki opened a brand-new factory at Toyokawa,

This is the bike that started Suzuki on the road to competition dominance – the RG500 works racer.

8

exclusively to produce motor cycles, to meet the tremendous demand from both the home and export markets.

The 'Selped' moped was one of the company's biggest sellers, and after a couple of years development, it was boosted to 80cc, and was to become one of the forerunners of Suzuki's best sellers of all time, the A100.

By the end of 1962, Suzuki had clinched their first World road racing Championship in the 50cc class, whilst in America, they were busy setting up their new headquarters under the 'U.S. Suzuki Motor Corporation' banner. The company decided that it needed to test its new prototype machines on a purpose-built track, so during 1962-3, it embarked on building its 5-mile Ryuyo test track near the factory.

Suzuki made steady progress in road racing, but in 1964 they surprised the road-race fans by entering into the world of moto cross Grands Prix. They entered the Japanese moto cross champion, Kazuo Kubo, in the Swedish 250cc Grand Prix, but without the same success they had achieved earlier in road racing. Although their machines were certainly fast enough, they did not handle well, so their engineers went back to the drawing board. Suzuki returned to Europe, the home of moto cross, in 1966 with completely redesigned machines, and found some success. In 1967 Suzuki signed up their first non-Japanese moto cross rider, the Swede, Olle Peterson.

But it was another European, the burly Joel Robert, who won Suzuki its first World Championship in 1970. Suzuki won again several times, and have won the 125cc class every year since its introduction in 1975.

October 1967 saw the launch of the 500cc Titan road machine. This was to be known throughout its 11-year production life as the Titan, the Charger and the Cobra, finishing its production run as the GT500. It was a 500cc twin-cylinder two-stroke, which despite its unusually long wheelbase, handled quite well and became highly popular.

The trail bike, with its on and off-road capabilities, was the big success story for all the Japanese manufacturers in the late 'sixties, and Suzuki launched their TS range, with knowledge gained from the moto cross World Championships, in March 1969.

But it was with two-stroke machines that Suzuki achieved their greatest successes, both on and off the tracks. They opened yet another factory in October 1969 at Toyama to produce small capacity two-strokes.

A machine which took the motor-cycling public and press by surprise was the astonishingly quick GT750 – a three-cylinder two-stroke capable of well over 110mph with acceleration to match. At 540lb, it was no lightweight, but its 67bhp pushed it to 60mph in only five seconds.

With the confidence gained from producing the large capacity GT750 two-stroke, Suzuki rejoined the racing scene when they announced to the world that they would campaign a totally new four-cylinder, two-stroke 500cc racer called the RG500. Quite simply, the RG500 was to

Suzuki's early four-cylinder production bikes lent themselves to being customised. This is the Paul Dunstall Special based on the GS1000.

become the single most successful racing machine of modern times, and by the time it had completed three full racing seasons it had clinched two World Championships with Britain's Barry Sheene aboard.

A model worthy of mention is the RE5. This was Suzuki's attempt at producing a rotary-engine machine. Based on the Wankel design from Germany, it proved to be a costly and expensive failure, and only 400 were sold in the UK.

Suzuki made a bold decision in 1976 to launch a range of four-stroke machines onto the world market, and these well-made and neatly styled machines were readily accepted by the motor-cycling public. The first machines were the GS400, a 400cc twin, and the potent four-cylinder 750cc GS750, with double-overhead camshafts.

The company then made tremendous headway with their four-stroke machines, introducing the powerful shaft-drive GS850G in October 1978. In an effort to create their own and completely new styling, Suzuki went to Europe to find a new look for a new and quite revolutionary range of 'Superbikes'. The new bikes were called 'Katana', and promised a performance and handling that was unknown on road-going machines before. Featuring Twin-Swirl combustion chambers and many other highly advanced technical features, the first Katana off the production line was the GS1000s.

March 1982, saw Suzuki's unveiling of their XN85 turbocharged 650cc superbike. This was the height of achievement for Suzuki's technical department, and although not yet widely on sale, promises to be a big seller, in Europe at least.

At the end of the 1982 road-racing season, Suzuki had once again clinched the 500cc road-racing World Championship, its eighth consecutive 125cc moto cross World Championship, and sixth 500cc moto cross World Championship. In September 1983, Suzuki announced 46 new models of motor cycles.

2 Road-going Lightweights

Suzuki's range of road-going lightweights, up to 400cc, at the end of the 'seventies was not very inspiring.

Yamaha were probably the most successful company selling light- to middle-weight, high-performance two-strokes, and their RD range was selling very well. The future of the two-strokes, in America at least, looked uncertain. American legislators were pushing tougher and tougher laws through the Senate, which meant that Suzuki would have to produce suitable bikes for their other world markets.

Although they did produce a hugely popular bike, the B100 'Student', which became a firm favourite with commuters and young riders wanting lively performance without too much expense, they felt that they had to produce a range of machines that would equal, if not better, their competitors in every way.

Mopeds and Scooters

The British laws concerning learner riders forced manufacturers to make smaller machines, which would not exceed 30mph, and which were, in fact, registered as mopeds.

A delightful little 50cc machine made its appearance at the end of 1979 – the GT50. The GT50 certainly didn't look like a moped with its big-like appearance, and it bore a striking resemblance to the larger GP125, despite the fact that it would reach only a fraction over 30mph with its 49cc engine.

Not everybody, however, wanted a sporting machine. There was still a huge, and partly untapped, market in bread-and-butter, get-to-work mopeds, and here Suzuki offered the FR80. This bike was designed many years ago to offer very cheap and reliable transport which was simple to operate, cheap to run and easy to maintain. It developed only 6.8bhp at 6500rpm, and had a three-speed gearbox and automatic clutch. It had built-in legshields, rather outdated styling, but was popular all the same.

Just a few months before the end of the decade, Suzuki gave a hint of what was to come from their smaller bike range. They launched a stylish little bike called the FZ50 which was soon to become known as the 'Suzy', and which was to become one of the company's biggest sellers for years. It was simplicity itself with its all-automatic transmission, twin carriers, 100-plus miles per gallon, and top speed of 30mph. It was cheap to insure and run, and sold for a surprisingly low £230.

Then, in 1980, with 'Chopper' style machines becoming the rage, Suzuki introduced a tiny 50cc moped, with radical chopper styling called the OR50. It had a raised seat, high-rise handlebars, 'tear-drop' style petrol tank and cast alloy wheels.

Another ultra-lightweight was the FS50, a 49cc single-cylinder scooter-type moped with carriers fitted front and back. In fact, scooters were making a very definite comeback, and Suzuki revealed their delightful little CS50 'Roadie' scooter-moped. This had the usual fully enclosed bodywork associated with a scooter, but it did not have the drawback of offering a dreadful ride on any but the smoothest surfaces. A thoroughly modern machine, it had an electric starter, flashing indicators, was fully automatic, had electronic ignition for total reliability, quick-change wheels, and was extremely cheap to insure and run.

In 1981, another 50cc moped chopper, the ZR50L, was announced, along with an updated version of the FR50, a 'Step-Thru' commuter-type moped with a spine frame and automatic, three-speed gearbox.

In 1983, Suzuki launched three new lightweights. One of their lightest ever machines, the CL50 Suzy Mark 2, known in Japan as the 'Love' made its first appearance in Britain. This is available either with a kickstart or electric starter, and is an ultra-modern scooterette with

She's called Suzy, she's pretty, and is a big hit with the ladies for shopping trips. Despite her uncluttered looks, Suzy's specification was quite sophisticated and would return over 120mpg.

14

two-speed automatic transmission, pressed-steel wheels, a built-in rear carrier and a host of other features.

With the Suzuki Suzy being a big hit, it was no surprise that the company launched a larger capacity version onto the market in 1983. Called the CS80D Roadie, it has a 79cc single-cylinder, two-stroke engine, with a three-speed automatic transmission, dual seat and pillion footrests, an electric starter, and weighs only 161lb. Many of the parts on the 79cc version are interchangeable with the earlier 50cc version.

For the younger section of the market, Suzuki will announce the exciting new lightweight ZR50SKX. The 50cc two-stroke, single-cylinder engine fitted into this new bike has been well tried in other Suzuki lightweights, so reliability is guaranteed. It has a stylish cockpit fairing, rev counter, dual seat, cast alloy wheels, disc brake, matt black exhaust, five-speed gearbox, and develops 2.9bhp at 6000rpm. No price is yet fixed for this model.

The 100-200cc Range

By 1979, Suzuki's range included eight models under 200cc.

Due to differences in insurance premiums, many younger riders were looking for a bike that would offer tremendous performance but would at the same time, be easier on their pockets than the bigger high-performance bikes. So Suzuki came up with a slightly smaller version of their highly successful GT250X7 (discussed on p. 22), the GT200X5. This was a brilliant marketing idea,

and the bike looked almost identical to its larger brother, with its distinctive styling. The smaller bike developed 20bhp at 8000rpm, and it had a five-speed gearbox, cast alloy wheels, one carburettor for each of its two cylinders, disc brakes, and weighed only 217lb.

There was also the commuter version, the SB200. This was not a stylish bike, but made for heavy-duty commuting with its single carburettor, drum brakes, four-speed gearbox, simple instrumentation and low state of tune. It was much slower than the GT200X5, but was much more economical and probably more reliable.

The FT185 was coming to the end of its life, with the GT200X5 coming too close for comfort. The GT185 was a lively and likeable twin-cylinder two-stroke with neat styling, good handling, disc brake, and developed 20bhp from its 184cc engine.

With the impending 125cc 'Learner Law' coming into force in the next few years, restricting machines in that class to no more than 12bhp, Suzuki, like other manufacturers, were, at the end of the 'seventies, thinking hard about the 125cc class.

In 1979, they had two excellent little 125cc bikes, the GT125 and the GP125. The GT version was the sportier of the two with its 16bhp being delivered at 9500rpm through its twin cylinders and twin carburettors. It had racy styling, a disc front brake, five-speed gearbox, and weighed only 238lb. The GP125 probably sold more, because it still delivered a very healthy 75mph from its 15bhp single-cylinder, two-stroke engine, and yet was more economical and

The 'Step-Thru' moped was a huge hit with ride-to-work motor cyclists who just wanted economy, simplicity, and reliability.

overleaf: *Responsive handling and zippy performance with reasonable economy were the hallmarks of the GT200X5 lightweight.*

possibly more reliable in its reduced state of tune. It was ideal for the young beginner with its tractable and forgiving nature. Later versions are on sale to this day, and it looks like becoming one of Suzuki's classic lightweights.

There were also two 100cc bikes in Suzuki's range at the end of the 'seventies. There was the GP100, a smaller capacity version of the GP125, and the A100. The A100 was clearly a different motor cycle from all the others. It used a spine-type frame, with its engine leaning forward at an angle. It used drum brakes, had a fully enclosed rear chain and was obviously designed with commuting in mind. It developed only 9.4bhp at

17

above: *Not everybody wanted a highly tuned two-stroke, so Suzuki produced the SB200 which was in a lower state of tune, and ideal for touring or commuting.*

right: *Popularly known as the 'Student', the Suzuki A100 lightweight was a big seller with riders who wanted fair performance with economy and reliability.*

7500rpm and, with its four-speed gearbox, was made to last rather than deliver high performance.

By 1982, Suzuki's Katana range of bikes in the larger capacity classes were selling well, so the company decided to make the most of the situation and launch a range of 125cc machines

to comply with the British government's new 125cc 'Learner Law' which was now in force.

A super-looking bike, the GS125E was the first to be announced. It had Katana styling, cast alloy wheels, a handlebar fairing, matt black exhaust and handled very well.

There was another 125cc machine with

similar, but not such radical, styling called the GS125. This used a drum brake on the front instead of a hydraulically operated disc, had wire-spoked wheels, more basic instrumentation, and was more spartan in appearance.

A prototype scooter of 125cc was also announced and is still to appear on the market. When it does, it will have a single overhead-camshaft, four-stroke engine, automatic three-speed transmission and an electric starter. The same four-stroke motor can be found in the DR125S trail bike.

The 250-450cc Range

Towards the end of the 'seventies, Suzuki were working behind the scenes to produce a new 250cc bike to replace their ageing GT250, which produced 'peaky' power, and was not the most manageable of bikes.

Perhaps the single most important machine Suzuki launched during this period was their much-hailed and controversial GT250X7. Much-hailed because of its performance, and controversial because many older riders felt it was too fast for the younger and less experienced riders. But legislation in Britain to prevent learners from riding a 250cc bike was not yet in force, and the bike soon found its way into the hands of young riders.

It was designed on a simple concept: make it as

Capable of 100mph, the GS425 was the successor to the GS400. A double overhead-camshaft, four-stroke twin, it handled and performed safely.

Suzuki had to compete in the 250cc market, and one of their latest bikes in this class was the GS250, a sweet – handling, high-performance, four-stroke twin.

light as possible, with highly responsive handling, good brakes, and offer the complete package as highly tuned as possible. It worked, and was a big seller. It used a 30bhp, twin-cylinder, two-stroke motor with a six-speed gearbox, twin carburettors, had electronic ignition, cast alloy wheels, and neat, clean styling. It was very fast, and was advertised as the 'Ton-Up' Suzuki. Whether it actually reached the magic 'ton' was arguable. The makers sold the bike on the promise that it would touch 100mph. It would, in the right hands, and in Suzuki's advertising leaflets, it was stated that it would reach between 98-104mph. It was certainly very fast and safe, and weighing in at only 282lb, was light and easy to throw into tight bends and corners.

A slightly smaller version, but almost identical in appearance, the GT200X5 was brought out soon after for the younger rider (see p. 16).

Trail bikes are a cross between a road bike and an off-road machine. Although ideal for normal road use, they can perform quite well on the rough with their knobbly tyres and low gearing.

Riders, in Europe at least, had had to make do with only one or two medium capacity four-strokes from the Japanese makers, so the 1976 GS400 twin-cylinder, double overhead-camshaft four-stroke was a welcome addition. It was quick, with a top speed of around 104mph, it handled well, was comfortable, fairly light, and soon gained a reputation as a speedy, reliable workhorse. The GS400 was developed in various frames, mostly styling variations and, with its 36bhp being obtained at 8800rpm, it was economical and easy to maintain. In 1978 it was given an extra 25cc's and renamed the GS425. It now had a six-speed gearbox and cast alloy wheels. It was further updated and improved, with a more powerful 40bhp engine, in 1979 when it became known as the GS425EN.

Another larger Suzuki was coming to the end of its production run by the late 'seventies. This

was the three-cylinder, two-stroke GT380. This bike was becoming outdated and outpaced when compared to the new breed of Suzukis' yet it performed well with its 37bhp motor. It used Suzuki's patented Ram-Air method of directing air to the cylinder heads, and had a six-speed gearbox.

Suzuki entered 1980 with a new zest and launched several new bikes. Their major new bike in the smaller capacity class was the superb and completely new GSX250. This was the company's first attempt at making a 250cc four-stroke and it looked as though they succeeded at first try. It used Suzuki's Twin Swirl Combustion Chamber design, with four valves per cylinder, twin overhead-camshafts, and twin carburettors to develop its 27bhp at a high revving 10000rpm. Hailed by many as perhaps the most advanced 250cc four-stroke to appear as a road machine, it became a firm favourite with its 90mph-plus top speed and over 50mpg capability.

A custom version, the FS250TT, and a semi-custom machine, the GN400 single-cylinder version were introduced soon after the GSX250.

Suzuki could see that the 400cc capacity range was an area of fast development, so in 1981, they launched two new 400cc models – a larger capacity version of the FSX250, the sporty GSX400, with four-cylinders, sixteen-valves and super performance, and the eight-valve GSX400T which was a twin-cylinder bike with more staid performance and styling.

With the craze for trail bikes increasing fast, Suzuki introduced this 50cc ultra-lightweight bike, the 50cc ER50 two-stroke single.

The Trail Bike Range

In America, off-road riding was becoming extremely popular, and all the Japanese manufacturers were producing suitable bikes. 'Trail' bikes soon became popular in Britain and Europe and now take a vast proportion of sales in the under-250cc market.

Suzuki offered an excellent range of dual-purpose road and off-road bikes, with the largest being the four-stroke SP370. A 369cc overhead-camshaft, single-cylinder bike, it produced a beefy 25bhp at 7500rpm, so cruising at a respectable speed was quite possible.

The TS250 was a 250cc two-stroke single, developing 23bhp, and the slightly smaller version, the TS185 developed 17bhp. Younger and less experienced riders could choose the TS125, or the TS100, with the 'moped' version, the TS50 being introduced at the end of 1979.

Although these bikes were perfectly capable of the job they were made for, they were just not stylish enough for the young buyers.

So the range was updated at the end of 1979 and the initials ERN were attached to several models, indicating that minor alterations had been incorporated.

Suzuki's plan in Britain for the future is to build on the models they already import rather than flood the market with new models which would mean a drop in second-hand prices of almost-new Suzukis.

3 Road-going Bigger Bikes and Superbikes

The 500-750cc Range

One of the most exciting machines ever built was announced by Suzuki in 1971. With Suzuki's success in two-stroke racing, it seemed quite natural for them to produce a powerful road-going two-stroke. This was the GT750, a full 750cc three-cylinder, two-stroke developing 67bhp at 6500rpm, and was to form the basis for Suzuki's incredibly fast 750cc road-racing machines which dominated 750cc road racing for a time. With a minimum amount of tuning, it could produce over 100bhp and touch close to 175mph.

Suzuki's engineers chose a three-cylinder two-stroke because they could use parts made for 250cc bikes and reduce the cost of expensive research and development. Rubber-mounted in the frame at eight points, it was water-cooled, which not only enabled the bike to be run for long periods at high speed, but kept it quiet mechanically. Water-cooling was also useful to keep the middle cylinder (the engine was an in-line three cylinder) cool – always a problem for three-cylinder machines – because it was partially masked by the frame and forks.

The GT750 was quite a sophisticated machine and had a four-stage cooling system. For quick warming up, the thermostat blanked off the outlet from the cylinder head to the radiator; at 82 degrees centigrade, the outlet to the radiator was opened; at 95 degrees the bypass was closed and all the water went through the radiator; but if the temperature got close to 105 degrees, an electric fan automatically cut in.

In its five-year production run, the 540lb, 112mph GT750 sold well despite a few of the problems usually associated with two-strokes. If its full power was used, with 0-60 available in five seconds, or it was ridden with heavy throttle hand, fuel economy suffered. It did, however, pave the way for the mighty TR750 racer, used successfully by Barry Sheene and others in the early 'seventies, but as a road machine, it gained a reputation for being fast, thirsty, and quite a handful at speed.

When the GT750 reached the end of its production run, it was replaced by an even more sophisticated and complex machine, the revolutionary RE5 Wankel-powered bike. Was it a two-stroke or a four-stroke? It was generally agreed that it was neither.

The Wankel, or rotary-engine, was not new, and when Suzuki launched the RE5 in 1974, many other firms, including Norton-Villiers, Triumph, Norton, the German Hercules, and Mazda and NSU, the car manufacturers, either had Wankels

The average road-going Superbike probably produces more power than a Grand Prix racing machine of only a few years ago, but has impeccable road manners.

on their drawing boards or actually on sale. But the RE5, with all its problems, was the first production Wankel-powered motor-cycle. Designed in the early 'fifties by a German engineer, Dr Felix Wankel, the single rotor machine was generally accepted as a 500cc machine, but as a 500cc bike, it was very heavy, ridiculously thirsty (between 20-40mpg) and left much to desire in the handling department. Weighing in at around 560lb when fully tanked up, problems included poor throttle response and, most important to potential buyers, it was complex and expensive to repair and maintain. By the time it was quietly withdrawn from the market in 1977, it had sold only 400 units in Britain, and it was never to appear again.

Even whilst the company was pushing the RE5 and, previously, the GT750, its engineers had, behind the scenes, been developing a new range of machines that were to change Suzuki's fortunes and image. Although they were still developing small-capacity two-strokes, they realised that in their biggest market, America, there were moves by the government to reduce pollution. The two-stroke was the biggest offender in this case, so they had to commit themselves to developing and selling four-strokes. Armed with the knowledge they had gained in the early 'fifties, they announced two totally new four-stroke machines in 1976 which took the motor-cycle enthusiasts and trade totally by surprise.

What was even more surprising was how good they were. There were two bikes – the GS400 twin-cylinder with a double overhead-camshaft, 400cc engine (see p.25), and the 750cc, four-cylinder GS750, also fitted with high-performance double overhead-camshafts.

The GS750 soon became a big seller, mainly because not only did it offer tremendously high performance, with top speed around 122mph, but was compact, handled well, had powerful disc brakes front and back, was attractively designed, and was quiet and refined. Handling was one of its biggest attractions because, up till now, most of the Japanese multi-cylinder machines were purely straight-line performers which were heavy and unwieldy when taken onto tight and twisty roads. It was also lighter, and the Japanese manufacturers realised that 'big' wasn't neccessarily good. In its various forms,

High insurance premiums meant that many riders could have been forced off the road, but Suzuki produced the power-packed GS550, a four-cylinder four-stroke with surprisingly good performance.

30

The craze for 'custom' bikes, with their different sized wheels, 'King and Queen' seat, and high-rise handlebars came in suddenly and stuck around. Many are still sold; this is the GS550L version.

the GS750 was to become one of the classic motor cycles of the 'seventies, not just from Suzuki, but from Japan. It set new standards in performance and sophistication and was considered *the* Japanese multi.

Not everyone, however was catered for by the GS750 and the GS400. Many wanted something in

between that would offer good performance without the weight of the larger bike, but with better touring comfort and features than the 400cc machine.

So the GS550 was born in 1977. Although it was somewhat overshadowed by the GS1000, the largest bike Suzuki had made to date which appeared at much the same time, the GS550 was good. It had double overhead-camshafts, making it quick for its class, with a top speed of around 112mph, and one of its many virtues was its fuel economy. It was not far short of the 750cc bike on

Considered to be one of the best-handling bikes in its class, the GSX750 combined race-bred handling with plenty of torquey power.

performance, but was much lighter on fuel. Its handling characteristics were popular with riders who wanted a bike not only for commuting but also for touring. Its 50bhp four-cylinder engine was matched to an excellent five-speed gearbox.

The GS550 and GS750 were both updated in 1978. 'Custom' styling, with raised handlebars, two-tier 'King and Queen' seat, small fat rear wheel, and cast alloy wheels, became fashionable around 1980, when Suzuki introduced their custom version of the GS550. It was called the GS550L, and although its styling was fairly radical, it still had the flexible and reliable four-cylinder engine developing 50bhp.

1980 was an important year for Suzuki, because it was the year it decided to launch two new bikes which were to confirm them as one of the leading manufacturers of high-performance motor cycles. These were the completely new GSX750 and GSX1100 machines.

Suzuki's research and development department had been hard at work behind the scenes developing a new design for the cylinder heads of the bikes which would take them into the 'eighties. Both the GSX750 and GSX1100 used Suzuki's 'Twin Swirl Combustion Chamber' or TSCC as it was to become known. The basic idea of the 16-valve head was that the small valves worked almost vertically in a shallow chamber, but where TSCC really scored was that in reshaping the combustion chamber it produced a fraction more power, and an engine 'cleaner' in terms of pollution control.

The styling of the GSX750 was quite different to anything Suzuki had tried before. It had a rectangular headlamp, large capacity fuel tank, completely new instrument panel with more comprehensive instrumentation, electric starting, cast alloy wheels, and it was quite obvious at first glance, that it was different from anything Suzuki had previously designed. Handling of the GSX750, which was a hefty machine at 510lb, was not the best in its class, but it could reach 120mph with its 80bhp motor.

1981 saw the introduction of the GS650G, and GS550M Katana-styled machines (for a description of this futuristic design, see p. 43); the GS650GT, and the GSX750E also continued for 1981 as well as the two 550cc bikes, the GS550L custom version, and the GS550E in standard trim.

The most dramatic machine by far of 1982 was the long-awaited XN85 Turbo. This was a

Advanced styling, 'Fully Floating', single damper rear suspension, and the latest small diameter wheels distinguish the newest GSX550ES four-cylinder bike.

The 1000cc four-cylinder overhead-camshaft GS1000 really put Suzuki on the Superbike map. To date, it has won countless titles in road racing and drag racing forms with its superb performance and ruggedness.

673cc four-cylinder, double overhead-camshaft bike, fitted with a turbocharger. Until fairly recently turbochargers were usually fitted only to drag racing bikes, but Suzuki had to follow the trend set by Honda with their cx500 Turbo, and produce such a machine. Its brake horsepower was not announced, but it was believed to be around 85 – more than enough for a bike weighing 444lb.

Press reports revealed that the xn85 was one of the finest-handling bikes ever to come out of Japan and, with its staggering performance, it looked set to repeat the success of the Katana, but without the weight and bulk of the larger bike.

Development on the turbocharged bike continues, but in 1983 Suzuki concentrated on other, less controversial machines, such as the 1983 gsx750es. This bike also uses the 16-valve, double overhead-camshaft, four-cylinder engine,

Although capable of over 130mph, the GSX1100 could be used for touring or commuting, but at the snap of the throttle, it would rocket from standstill to 60mph in under four seconds.

but is of 747cc and develops 83bhp at 9500rpm. It uses Suzuki's Full Floating rear suspension which utilises one large shock absorber mounted behind the engine and is said to be an improvement on the traditional twin-shock system. It also has a square-section tubed frame, the design of which is based on the RG500 Grand Prix racing bike. It is said to offer greater rigidity, and, therefore, greater road-holding. It has a 16-in. front wheel and anti-dive front forks. A top-half fairing is fitted, along with cast alloy wheels.

An exceptionally good looking bike in the 1983 range is the GSX550ES, hailed by Suzuki as 'The Sports Machine Of 1983'. Its advanced specification includes the 16-valve engine, a six-speed gearbox, 16-in. front wheel and anti-dive front forks, square-section frame, Full Floating rear suspension, and a twin-choke carburettor. Its 572cc four-cylinder engine develops a healthy

61bhp at 9500rpm, and weighing only 406lb is very fast indeed.

The 850-1000cc Range

Up till 1977, the handling of the 1000cc bikes from Japan was no match for the British Triumphs and Nortons, and the Italian sports machines, but the arrival on the scene of the GS1000 was to change all that. According to the press, it was the answer motorcyclists had been waiting for, and it was certainly to change Suzuki's image and its fortunes.

Here was a Japanese bike that at last not only performed well, but its 90bhp, developed at 8500rpm, could be used to the full, thanks to its superb frame and suspension design.

Weighing in at around 516lb empty, it was one of the lightest 1000cc machines to come out of Japan, and was lighter than some 750s. It still used the immensely strong double-cradle frame, and braking was provided by two massive hydraulic discs at the front and one at the rear.

The GS1000 was immediately taken up by riders all over the world and used for competition. With its built-in handling properties, it was used in production racing in America, South Africa, Australia and Britain, and it also became popular with drag racers here in Britain, America and in Sweden.

By 1978, the GS1000 had been updated, and a new addition made to the range of 1000cc machines. Although using the same power plant, the new bike looked quite different. Called the GS1000s, it now had a small 'bikini' handlebar fairing, cast alloy wheels which not only looked good but reduced the unsprung weight, and additional instruments, including a clock, oil temperature gauge and an accessory terminal. Also included in the specification were air-assisted front forks which could be adjusted to suit the riders' needs. It was made available in two colour schemes – either blue and white or red and white.

The standard GS1000 continued unchanged, outwardly at least, for 1978, but with so much power being put through a rear chain, Suzuki's engineers began to look at other ways of transmitting the power. The answer was not new. Shaft-drive had been around for many years, most well-known in the German BMWs and the British Sunbeam of the 'fifties, but Suzuki felt they should offer shaft-drive as an alternative in their range, not to change over completely to shafts.

The GS850, as it was to be called, was a bit of a hybrid. It incorporated some of the best features of the GS750, and others from the GS1000 and GS1000s. Shaft-drive offered greater smoothness in operation, longer wear of engine parts and rear tyre, needed virtually no maintenance, reduced power loss to a minimum, and made transmission jerk a thing of the past. It was an immediate success, and as Suzuki's first attempt at shaft-drive, was an engineering feat, with its built-in shock absorber in the drive unit. The GS850 was no sluggard; it developed 77bhp at 8500rpm, but was thought of more as a fast tourer than an out-and-out sports bike. It, too, had cast alloy wheels, and updated styling, but was quite heavy at 557lb dry.

Suzuki's flagship is the mighty GSX1100S Katana, named after a Samurai warrior's sword. Lightning performance with incredible handling makes this an expert's machine.

Suzuki's large-capacity, four-cylinder four-strokes were an ideal base for the many companies throughout the world who offered 'bolt-on' accessories which would make Suzukis look faster and go faster. One such company was the British Paul Dunstall concern. After examination of its products and services, Heron Suzuki, the British importers of Suzuki, decided to make Dunstall their official manufacturer of special tuning equipment and customising accessories. Dunstall's products were made for many of the larger capacity Suzukis, but concentrated mostly on the GS1000.

With Dunstall's hi-performance camshafts, large-bore carburettors, high-compression pistons, tuned four-into-two exhaust system, the GS1000 would touch over 150mph, helped, of course, by a Dunstall full fairing. Other accessories for the GS1000 included race-style seats, handlebars, sports mudguards and racing-style petrol tanks. The 'Dunstall Suzuki 759GT', fitted with its full kit, would reach 135mph, and cover the standing quarter-mile in 12 seconds – very impressive.

Later in 1979, the GS850 shaft-drive bike was updated and called the GS850N, but in 1980, Suzuki decided to put shaft-drive into the GS1000.

Many owners were finding that their rear drive chains were being destroyed at an alarming rate, and needed constant adjustment due mainly, because of the tremendous power that was being transmitted through them. The GS1000 continued in its chain driven form, the ET. Developing 90bhp, it was good for 130mph, had air-assisted suspension, and handled very well. With its four carburettors, it could reach up to 45mpg, quite an achievement for such a potent machine.

The 1000cc-plus Range

By 1980 competition in the 1000cc-plus class was getting white hot. Honda had their flagship, the six-cylinder, 24-valve, 140mph, 105bhp, 560lb, CBX which would touch 100mph in under nine seconds, and 60mph in three. Kawasaki had their behemoth, the Z1300 – a true monster of a machine, which weighed a staggering 684lb with one gallon of fuel, would hit over 137mph, accelerate from standstill to 60mph in a fraction over three seconds, and still return a best fuel consumption figure of around 48mpg.

Yamaha, one of Suzuki's fiercest competitors on the race track, were selling their heavy, but powerful 1100cc XS1100. This was quite an under-rated machine which although did not handle too well, would still touch 100mph in 12

The 1983 GSX1100ES is a real road-burner and one of the fastest accelerating machines ever made. This model features a new frame and fairing to combat high-speed wind resistance.

seconds, hit a top speed of 130mph, and return a best fuel consumption figure of 40mpg-plus. The Yamaha was really at its best touring on the open road.

So Suzuki had to produce a machine that had at least to compete on even terms with the other bikes on offer from their Japanese counterparts. Their GSX1100 seemed to answer all their prayers. It incorporated the TSCC system, would deliver its 99bhp at 8700rpm at an alarming rate, yet soon gained a reputation for predictable handling and smooth, and effortless power. In short, it was the machine that Suzuki had wanted to sell for many years.

Its performance was quite simply staggering. For a 99bhp machine to be capable of being launched to the all-important 0-60mph in exactly three seconds was impressive enough, but it would also reach nearly 137mph in the right conditions, and return a best fuel consumption figure of nearly 48mpg. The GSX1100 wasn't too heavy either, at 537lb including one gallon of fuel.

With handling and sheer performance well up to the standards of the other superbikes' manufacturers, Suzuki spent much time and research making sure that items such as lighting, braking, and rider comfort of this machine were also of a high standard. The large rectangular headlamp was of the quartz halogen type; there were three hydraulically assisted disc brakes fitted; and on the 'dashboard' there was a silhouette of the entire machine. Whenever a light 'blew', the built-in electronic sensors would flash up onto the silhouette, giving the rider ample warning.

With its massive performance, the GSX1100 was still a forgivable, but very large, motor cycle. Engine flexibility was one of its charms, and it could be trickled along in top gear as low as 30mph, but snapping the throttle open would rocket the bike to over 70mph in four and a half seconds.

Meanwhile, the builders of special high-performance machines were busy behind the scenes, and one in particular, Bimota, was making the most of Suzuki's engineering. Bimotas were hand-built, high-performance machines designed purely for the rider who wanted the ultimate in out-and-out performance and handling, and was prepared to pay for the privilege. Bimota, imported into Britain by David Dixon Racing of Godalming in Surrey, would make Bimotas available in various forms, depending on the customers' budget. Even in 1980, their top performer would touch close to 150mph with the GS1000 power plant fitted and cost close to £5000.

Whilst the large capacity Suzukis were selling well enough world-wide, Suzuki Japan looked to Europe for its next, and probably most exciting, project. A former BMW car designer, Jan Fellstrom, was running a design company in Germany, and it was to him that Suzuki turned for inspiration for the design of the bike that would ensure total domination of the fast-growing 'Superbike' market.

Suzuki's engineer's had developed an immensely powerful version of their four-cylinder, 16-valve double overhead-camshaft engine which would produce a staggering 111bhp at 8500rpm. What it needed was a different type of design, and a new look. Not just by adding a fairing or changing the shape of the fuel tank, but something that would really stand out from the crowd.

Fellstrom met with Suzuki's engineers and using their race-bred twin duplex frame, he came up with a futuristic design which was to be called the 'Katana' after a sword used by Samurai warriors. Built for the experienced and skilful rider, mainly in Europe, the Katana offered incredible acceleration with a 0-100mph capability of around eight seconds, a top speed close to 140mph, reasonable fuel economy, and excellent road holding and road manners.

The Katana was equally happy trundling along in traffic as it was cruising at over 100mph on motorways. It had a sporting riding position, a fly-screen, clip-on handlebars, rear-set footrests, and futuristic instrument layout. Not only was it fast, but it was reliable with its transistor electronics and 12-volt electrical system.

Meanwhile, the GSX1100 became the 'E' version and using the same basic plant as the Katana, it offered a more practical means of delivering its 99bhp. Its air-assisted suspension with the rear adjustable to nine different positions offered a comfortable ride under any road conditions.

By the end of 1981, Suzuki had five machines of 1000ccs or over in their range, including the GSX1100 Katana, GSX1100E, GSX1000S Katana, GS1000G shaft drive, and the GS1000E.

1982 saw even more exciting machinery from Suzuki. They introduced the less dramatic GSX1100EZ which although it developed 111bhp did not have Katana styling, and continued with the large capacity Katanas.

Their big new bike in this class for 1983 was the handsome GSX1100ES, which uses the immensely powerful, 111bhp 16-valve, four-cylinder engine. Looking quite different from previous Suzukis, it has a half-fairing, halogen headlight, and inherits the superb handling characteristics of the Katana. An important development included in the specification of the GSX1100ES is anti-dive front forks. When a motor cycle is braked hard, the weight bias changes, and in extreme cases, the front wheel can break adhesion with the road surface. The Suzuki anti-dive system is said to eliminate this problem, and is a direct development from the racing machines.

4 Sporting Bikes

With many road racing and off-road World Championships to its credit, Suzuki is one of the most successful companies ever to compete in motor-cycle sport. In particular, their square-four, two-stroke RG500 road racing machine is perhaps the single most successful racing machine to have been produced in Japan, and maybe in the history of road racing.

In the rough and tumble world of moto cross, they have won several World Championships, with Belgian Roger de Coster winning no less than five 500cc world titles on a Suzuki. In the 125cc moto cross class, Suzuki have won the championship every year since it began in 1975.

Suzuki have also been successful in trials, with their solo and sidecar machines taking many championships and important events. Although their trials machines, which were made in Sussex, are no longer produced, they are now changing hands at more than they cost new, such is their popularity.

Road Racing

The RG500 is the star of their racing stables, and it has won countless championships in many countries throughout the world.

Britain's Barry Sheene has won two World Championships, in 1976 and 1977 with the incredibly fast RG500. Originally designed in the early 'sixties, the RG500 was soon the choice of top riders everywhere, and it was available, at a price, over the counter in many countries.

Despite Yamaha taking the World Championships in the 500cc class, the winning machines were chased home each time by hordes of RG500s. Britain's Isle of Man TT races held in June each year, provided the real test of the RG500 with their tight and tortuous bends and hills. The bike had to touch speeds up to 180mph, cope with 20mph hairpin bends, withstand the tremendous bumps and jarrs that a pure road circuit produced, and yet be utterly reliable over several hours of racing. Many riders believed that the RG500 was the best all-round machine for the Isle of Man TT circuit.

The cylinders of the RG500 were in a square-four formation, which was quite a brave move on the part of Suzuki, because ten years before they had failed dismally with a 250cc square-four racing machine. And the early days of the RG500 were fraught with problems, both in the power plant and handling departments. Developing around 115bhp and weighing about 315lb, it was extremely fast, with top speed in the region of

This is one of the later RG500 Grand Prix machines without its full fairing. Developing incredible horsepower, the 'works', or factory-prepared, machines will hit speeds up to 185mph, and have taken several riders to a World Championship.

180mph. But it suffered from ignition and carburation problems from the outset. Handling was said to be quite frightening on the earlier versions.

By 1976, however, most of the problems were ironed out, thanks in part to the efforts of an East German engineer, Ernst Degner. Degner defected to the West in 1961 and joined the Suzuki factory, where he used to great effect his skills as an engine designer and tuner perfected at the MZ factory.

Eventually, the RG500 was readily available over the counter – but at a price. Early models changed hands for close to £8000 each! But the factory were not foolish enough to have the production bikes too similar to the 'works', or factory machines. They were always one step ahead, and despite many privateers tinkering with their bikes, they did not have the edge that the factory machines had.

45

The development on the RG500 continues to this day, and the machines that can be bought over the counter are probably as fast and sophisticated as the early factory bikes.

Moto Cross

If Suzuki are successful in road racing, then their success in off-road events is spectacular. In moto cross, the roughest and toughest of the off-road sports, Suzuki have had incredible success, winning, for example, the 125cc World Championship ever since it began in 1975.

Like most branches of motor-cycle sport, ideas incorporated in the works bikes eventually find their way to the road machines, and with the increase in popularity of 'trail' bikes, Suzuki's success in off-road competition was becoming increasingly important to them.

Development in the 125cc class rocketed ahead more than in any other class of the sport. Weight was one of the major factors that designers concentrated upon. With the world governing body of motor-cycle sport, the Fédération Internationale Motorcycliste, imposing weight limits on the machines, engineers had to try to balance power-to-weight and power-to-fuel capacity ratios. If they got the balance wrong, their machines might produce tremendous power but use up too much fuel, which could mean that the machine would not be able to finish a Grand

Probably the best-known British rider in recent years, Barry Sheene poses with his new RG500 racer. A similar bike took him to two World Championships in 1976/77.

Prix on the permissable amount of fuel carried.

Engineers also pruned weight by using lighter and more specialised materials, such as magnesium. But due to the expense of the metals, they were not incorporated in the production bikes. With the little 125cc engines being ridden flat out for a total of 90 racing minutes each day, cooling was a problem. Suzuki's technical department experimented with water-cooled cylinder heads and barrels, and they eventually appeared on the works bikes in Grands Prix. Water-, or liquid-cooling allowed the works riders to keep their machines revving much higher and longer, and therefore keep Suzuki at the top of its class. Other manufacturers followed suit, but Suzuki kept their lead and total superiority in the 125cc class.

The other main area of development in moto cross was suspension and, with machines producing more and more power, the suspension was soon being worked to its limits. Suzuki's engineers and research and development department had to do something dramatic. They came up with a single massive suspension unit that would eventually replace the traditional twin shock absorber system, which had been in use for many years.

Although Suzuki were not the first to use single-shock rear suspension their 'Fully Floating' system as it was to be called, was successful from the start. It enabled the machines to be hurled into seemingly impossible handling situations and not only survive, but exit the turn or bend faster than the other bikes. The 125cc production Suzuki moto crosser was the first to benefit from Fully Floating suspension, and it

was successful very quickly in America and Europe, where 125cc racing is more popular, with adults at least, than in Britain.

Suzuki were also very successful in the next largest class of moto cross, 250cc, where Belgian Georges Jobe reigned supreme for a year or two.

It was another Belgian, Roger de Coster, known as 'Mr Moto Cross', who gave Suzuki its greatness in moto cross, winning a record five 500cc World Championships for Suzuki.

The most spectacular, and certainly the fastest, of the off-road sports, 500cc Grand Prix moto cross is the most prestigious class too, and is the area where most of the research and development budgets are spent. The latest factory works bikes develop over 60bhp, which for a machine weighing around 220lb, or 100kg, is incredible. This produces thrilling and sometimes 'hairy' racing. Suzuki were beaten in the 500cc class for several years until American Brad Lackey took them to victory in 1982, and became America's first-ever World 500cc Champion at the same time.

Trials and Enduro

The slowest, and arguably the least spectacular, of off-road sports, is trials. Here again, Suzuki were successful, winning many championships. But Suzuki's first efforts into trials machine manufacture was a dismal failure.

This is the over-the-counter production RM500 bike with the new 'Full Floating' rear suspension.

Suzuki factory trials machines were unsuccessful until they were radically altered by an Englishman, Graham Beamish. They were eventually to be re-exported to Japan!

This is the GS1000 in its standard form, but when race-tuned, it won many important races in America, Europe and Australasia.

In 1971, they produced a single-cylinder, 250cc two-stroke, and signed Gordon Farley, a top British rider, to ride their trials bike for them. Although he met with a certain measure of success, Suzuki never really achieved their aim to become World Champion manufacturers. An Englishman, Graham Beamish, was the importer

for Suzuki moto cross machines in the early 'seventies, and it was he who was to set the record straight and produce a complete turn-around in Suzuki's trials efforts.

He was sent a batch of Suzuki's trials bikes for evaluation, and set to work on them. Within a few months he had changed the machine radically and made an offer to Suzuki in Japan to buy the

51

remaining stocks of their trials bikes.

They were only too pleased to get rid of them, and so successful was Beamish that he eventually sold nearly 1600 of them, 1500 to Europe alone. So popular were the Beamish-based machines that two were sold back to Japan, and a shrewd Japanese businessman has bought up all the remaining stocks of machines from Beamish and now sells them world-wide! Several versions were made of the Beamish-based Suzuki, including 325cc models, and sidecar machines. One model, the 'works' Beamish RL325, weighed only 160lbs and was super-competitive.

In America, a new off-road sport was developing using a hybrid machine based on a moto cross bike, but with the addition of lights, and a rudimentary silencer. The sport, Enduro, was already popular in Europe, and in Italy in particular, where there were already classes for Enduro machines from 50cc upwards.

The machine Suzuki finally offered over the counter was the PE250, a 250cc single-cylinder two-stroke, very highly tuned, and in the hands of less experienced riders quite difficult to handle. But ridden by top experts, it was to be spectacularly successful, particularly in Britain.

Later, a 175cc version, the PE175 was produced, and this was eventually to outsell the larger version by about ten to one.

It is in the past two years or so, that the PE range has had any serious competition from other Japanese manufacturers, and it is truly a classic competition motorcycle.

Endurance Events and Drag Racing

With large-capacity, multi-cylinder road machines becoming more and more popular, Suzuki entered into long-distance endurance events using first, their GS750 and then GS1000 machines to great effect. Many riders believed the GS1000 to be one of the best-handling of the big machines to come out of Japan, and it enjoyed successes in many different countries.

Drag racing was another area where the four-cylinder GS1000 made quite an impression. An Englishman, Pip Higham, was partly sponsored by Suzuki in Britain to drag race his extremely fast GS1000-based bike. He took the bike, in its various versions, to many excellent wins in the 'Street Bike' class.

5 Junior Bikes

Several world motor-cycle champion, mostly off-road champions, started riding at a very early age, often as young as five or six years old, and owe their championships to the experience gained from years of practice.

Until fairly recently, the only machines a youngster could ride were either special home-made bikes, or full-size machines, usually off-road, with considerable risk of injury. Suzuki have probably been responsible for introducing more youngsters into motor-cycle competitions with their trials and moto cross machines, than any other Japanese manufacturer.

Rules and regulations for junior sport vary from country to country, but one thing is certain: the younger a rider starts, the better his chances of success in later years. Two former World Champions, Britain's Neil Hudson and Graham Noyce, both started competing in moto cross when they were very young, and became 250cc and 500cc World Champions respectively. When Noyce clinched his World Championship in 1979, he had been racing for around 14 years! This gave him the edge on European riders who rarely start racing until their early teens.

Suzuki's smallest off-road machines – they do not make junior road racing bikes as there is no suitable class available – are 50cc moto crossers. It would be a mistake to think that these tiny machines with single-cylinder, two-stroke motors are made just for riding around the garden. They are purpose-made, race-tuned and highly sophisticated miniature racing machines, which could throw off even an experienced adult rider who dared to underestimate it.

In Britain, boys and girls can start riding in special junior moto cross events at the age of six. Called the Cadet class, the bikes used have four- or five-speed gearboxes, and the Suzuki machine, the RM50, developed a healthy 8bhp at 10,000rpm, was fitted with 14in. front tyres and 12in. rear, and weighs a fairly hefty 123lb.

Once the youngster reaches a certain age, he is then obliged to compete in a larger capacity class, with machines up to 80cc being allowed. In fact, so popular is the 80cc class, that from 1984 onwards, youngsters will start to compete on 60cc machines, then go straight on to 80cc bikes.

Because not all young riders are built the same, and vary in height and weight, Suzuki took the step a couple of years ago of offering their two 80cc moto cross bikes in two different frame sizes. Their RM80XD machine develops an undisclosed bhp figure from its 79cc two-stroke, single-cylinder engine, and has smaller wheels than its larger brother. Both have six-speed gearboxes, and are extremely fast and competitive. The RM80XHD has a larger frame and wheels, although it uses the same engine and similar cycle parts. Both machines incorporate Suzuki's latest suspension technology and are fitted with the company's 'Fully Floating' single-shock rear suspension system.

The schoolboy moto cross classes range from 60cc (as from this year; previously they began at 50cc), 80cc, 100cc, and 125cc and, of course, Suzuki make machines suitable for all these classes.

Due to the length of moto cross races, two-stroke engines can be subject to overheating, so Suzuki include water cooling on many of their junior bikes, with the exception of the 50cc bike. A young rider could in theory, start his racing career on a 50cc machine, and go through all the junior classes – 80cc, 100cc, right up to the maximum class allowed in junior sport, the 125cc class.

British riders, when they reach the age they have to leave junior moto cross and race with adults, usually prefer to go to 250cc or even 500cc class racing. On the continent, however, this is

above: *Make no mistake, the 80cc schoolboy moto cross machine is a really competitive machine. This model is made in two frame sizes – this is the larger version. Suzuki moto cross bikes have probably won more championships than any other machine and, until recently, had won every 125cc World Championship since the class was started.*

left: *Strictly not for the children! Grand Prix rider Randy Mamola wheelies a 50cc moto cross bike designed for six-year-olds who can legally compete in moto cross at that age. These purpose-built machines are not toys, but highly tuned competition machines.*

not the case, and there has yet to be a British adult world 125cc champion.

So, it is quite possible for a rider to begin racing on a 50cc Suzuki and reach the peak of his career on a 500cc Suzuki. In the top junior class, 125cc, Suzuki have won the World Championship every year since its inception.

6 Star Riders

Wherever there is motor-cycle competition Suzuki will be represented to one degree or another. They have plenty to be proud about in motor-cycle competition and have won countless championships including world titles in both road racing and moto cross.

Their line-up for 1983 was quite formidable, and included the World 500cc road-racing Champion, Italian Franco Uncini, and Britain's former double World Champion, Barry Sheene. Suzuki were also the holders of the World 500cc moto cross Championship, the sport's most prestigious title, which was won by American Brad Lackey in 1982.

Road Racing

It is, however, road racing which pulls the crowds and gets most of the attention. From 1978 to 1980 American Kenny Roberts held the World Championship title on his factory Yamaha, but his seemingly impregnable hold was finally broken in 1981 by Marco Lucchinelli. Italy had been having a lean time with World Champions in motor-cycle sport, so it was a great delight when Franco Uncini took the 1982 title. Another Italian, Loris Reggiani rode a standard production Suzuki RG500 in 1983. He did, however, use his machine fitted with a very special frame, which proved to be an advantage over the 'works' bikes.

A German, Toni Mang, also rode in the Grands Prix on a factory-prepared machine. Mang, a fiercely competitive rider, was formerly World 350cc and 250cc Champion, so had plenty to offer the factory team. He was joined in the same team, sponsored by a cigarette company, by a young American, Randy Mamola.

Mamola, who rode for the British Suzuki importers for several years, never quite lived up to everyone's expectations, and despite some very close shaves with the World Championships, never quite made it. A protégé of Kenny Roberts, Mamola is a small, but tough competitor who started his racing career in America at the grand old age of fourteen! Rumours were rife that Mamola would leave Suzuki and join another Japanese factory team, but he rode a full-works machine in 1983.

Britain was well represented in the Grands Prix by Suzuki riders. Leading the team was Barry Sheene, now 32 years old, but his great

The stocky American rider, Randy Mamola, started racing in America at the age of fourteen!

above: *The young American Randy Mamola was a protégé of multi-World Champion and fellow American, Kenny Roberts. His hard riding style is much liked by the racegoers.*

right: *Horrific injuries still haven't knocked Barry Sheene off his pedestal so far as the fans are concerned, and this popular rider has two world crowns to his credit, both achieved on Suzukis.*

determination means that he must always be considered as a serious contender for the world title in the 500cc class. Sheene won his World Championships in 1976 and 1977 on a works Suzuki, but left a couple of years ago to ride Yamahas.

It was on a Yamaha that he had a horrific accident in 1982 which many believed would finally end his long and successful career. Sheene, who was nearly killed in a spectacular crash in Daytona several years ago on a Suzuki, has fought back from injury once again, but rode a

production RG500 racer fitted with special parts for the early part of the 1983 season and finished the season on a full-works bike. Factory machines have special tuning and parts which give an edge over production machinery, ensuring that a privateer will not beat a factory-backed rider.

Sheene rides in the Grands Prix with several inches of metal plates, rods and screws in his arms and legs, and such is his determination that he was water-skiing in South Africa only a few months after his crash in practice for the British Grand Prix at Silverstone two years ago.

above: *Sporting his famous Number 7, Barry Sheene pulls a victory wheelie after winning a race on a Suzuki.*

right: *The rough and tumble sport of moto cross produces some spectacular riding as seen here with British rider Jeremy Whatley flying high into the air.*

He was backed up in the British Suzuki team by 26-year-old Keith Huewen. He has had a very successful couple of seasons, and in 1983 he contested the British Championship rounds mainly, and a few Grands Prix. Depending how well he goes during the earlier part of next season, he might be offered the chance to race in more Grands Prix.

Formula 1 racing is very popular and Suzuki have been tremendously successful in this class.

They had a crack team to ride in Formula 1 in Britain, with veteran Mick Grant, the oldest member of the team at 37, leading the onslaught. Grant is more experienced in Formula 1 than any other rider in the Suzuki team, and also contested other major British events, including the Isle of Man TT races, where he has won many times.

A newcomer to Suzuki is 24-year-old Rob McElnea who will also ride Formula 1 Suzukis in British events. This hard-riding man is expected

to do very well indeed, and his determination on and off the track is very impressive.

Moto Cross

Although it does not have the same following as road racing, moto cross is a fast-moving, spectacular sport which is growing in popularity.

Suzuki were world title holders in the 500cc class in 1982, with American Brad Lackey winning the championship for them last year after years of back-breaking struggle. Sadly, Brad has left Suzuki, and the team leadership went to the Belgian André Vromans. A small, and highly talented rider, Vromans has yet to win the title, but that is not for lack of trying. If ever a man deserved a title for sheer ability, courage, and persistence, it would go to Vromans.

Some riders are good in certain conditions, and Vromans is acknowledged by all, including other Grand Prix riders, to be the world's best sand rider. He also goes extremely well in other conditions, but if all the Grands Prix were held in sandy conditions, Vromans would be unbeatable.

In the 250cc class, another Belgian, Georges Jobe, led the Suzuki team in the 1982 Grands Prix. In his early twenties, the stocky Jobe has two world titles to his name, and is a talented and skilled rider on all types of terrain. His style has come in for criticism from some quarters where it is felt that he gives other riders less than enough room on the track, and that occasionally he should be reprimanded for his riding. The fact remains that he is a good man to lead the team.

The 125cc class virtually belongs to Suzuki, who have won it every year since its inception. Although not hugely popular in England, where 125cc bikes are usually ridden by schoolboys, this capacity is extremely popular in Europe and America, where sales of this class of bike are important to the manufacturers. The team leader was yet another Belgian, Eric Geboers, younger brother of another famous rider, Sylvain Geboers. Eric is a fine rider, and was a firm favourite to win the 1983 World 125cc Championship.

Britain's top Suzuki rider is a youngster called Jeremy, or 'Jem', Whatley. A tall, slim rider, his appearance belies a fierce and spectacular style of riding. Whatley will get a full-works bike in the 250cc class, and will race in all the Grands Prix and major British Championships. Many followers of moto cross feel that Whatley is possibly Britain's best hope of a 250cc championship since the last champion, Neil Hudson.

Drag Racing

Another area of sport where Suzuki are to continue is drag racing. Britain's Pip Higham has been campaigning a high-tuned, 1000cc Suzuki for some years now, with great success. He is well known on the dragstrips of Britain and Europe in the spectacular sport and is expected to collect more championships again this year.

150mph in under 10 seconds is the order of the day in drag racing, even on a bike that started life as a standard machine. This is Britain's Pip Higham.